PIANO VOCAL GUITAR

LINKIN PARK A THOUSAND SUNS

W9-BZS-056

2 THE REQUIEM

6 BURNING IN THE SKIES

14 WHEN THEY COME FOR ME

24 ROBOT BOY

31 JORNADA DEL MUERTO

34 WAITING FOR THE END

43 BLACKOUT

52 WRETCHES AND KINGS

59 WISDOM, JUSTICE, AND LOVE

62 IRIDESCENT

70 FALLOUT

72 THE CATALYST

85 THE MESSENGER

ISBN 978-1-61774-296-5

HAL•LEONARD®
CORPORATION

7777 W. BLUEMOUND RD. P.O. BOX 13819 MILWAUKEE, WI 53213

Visit Hal Leonard Online at
www.halleonard.com

THE REQUIEM

Words and Music by CHESTER BENNINGTON,
ROBERT BOURDON, BRAD DELSON,
DAVE FARRELL, JOSEPH HAHN
and MIKE SHINODA

Atmospherically

God save us, ev-'ry - one, ___ will we burn ___

___ in - side the fire of a thous - and suns? ___ For the sins ___

___ of our hand, sins ___ of our tongue, sins ___

___ of our fa - thers and sins ___ of our young?

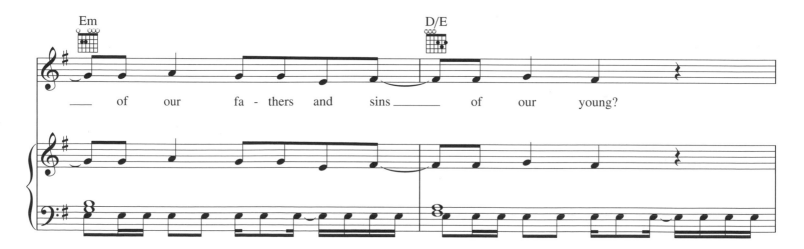

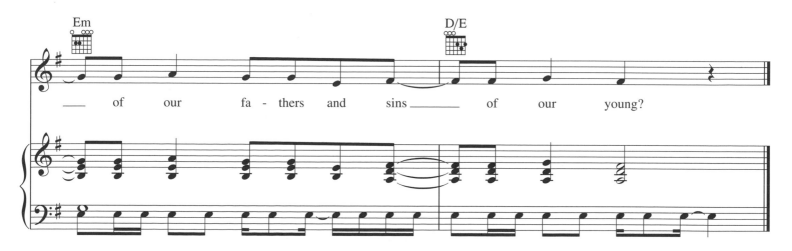

BURNING IN THE SKIES

Words and Music by CHESTER BENNINGTON,
ROBERT BOURDON, BRAD DELSON,
DAVE FARRELL, JOSEPH HAHN
and MIKE SHINODA

Pop Rock

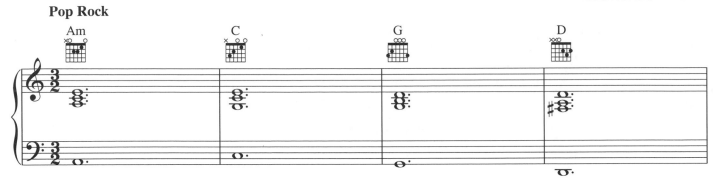

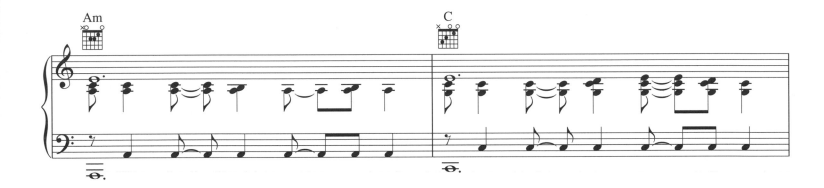

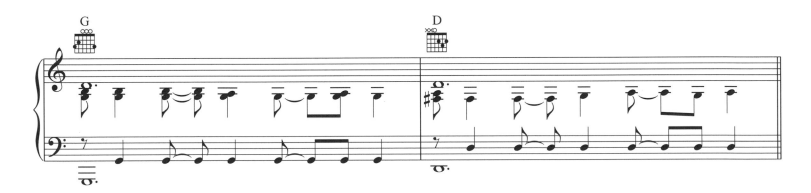

I used the dead - wood to make the fi - re rise,
We held our breath when the clouds be - gan to form,

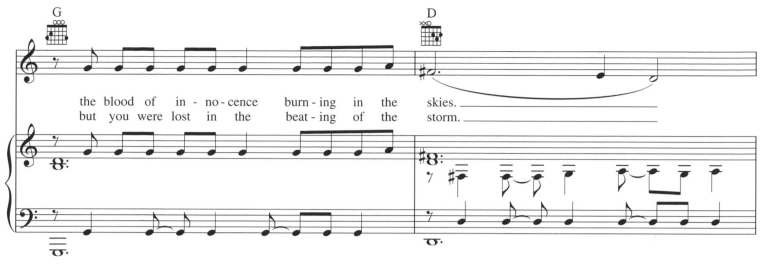

the blood of in-no-cence burn-ing in the skies. _____
but you were lost in the beat-ing of the storm. _____

I filled my cup with the ris-ing of the sea,
And in the end, we were made to be a - part,

I poured it out in an o-cean of de-bris. _____
the sep-'rate cham - bers _ of the hu - man heart. _____

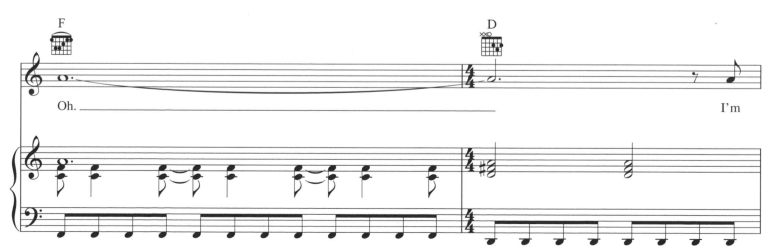

Oh. _____ I'm

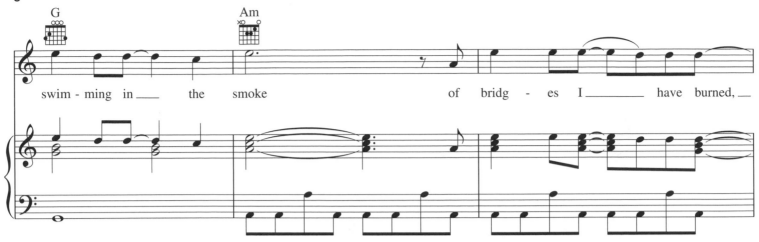

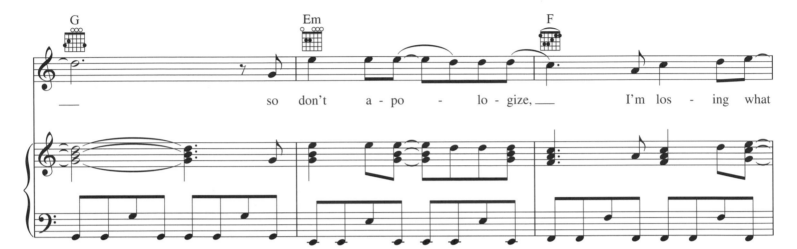

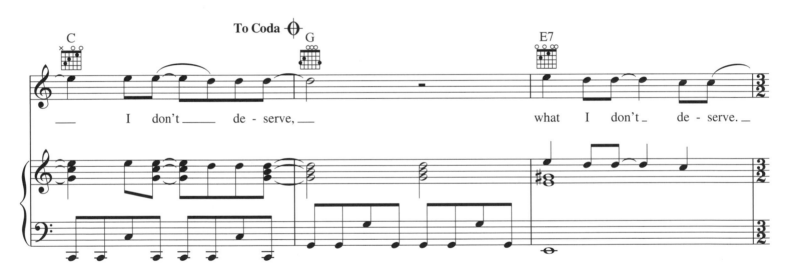

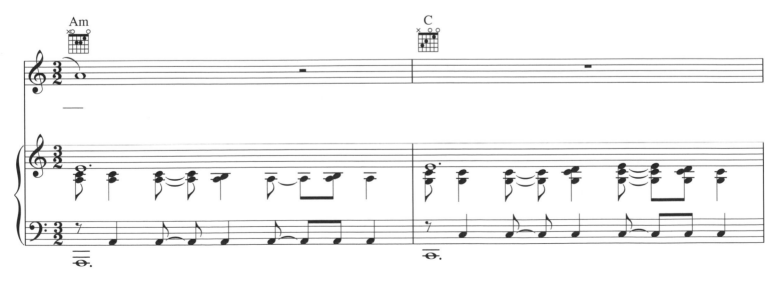

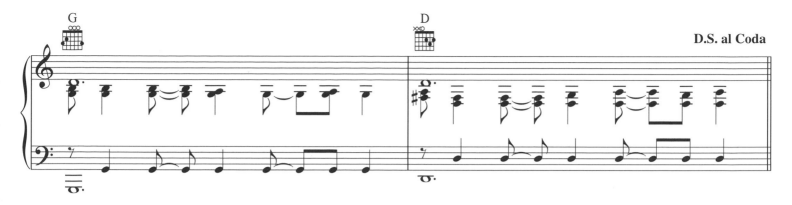

D.S. al Coda

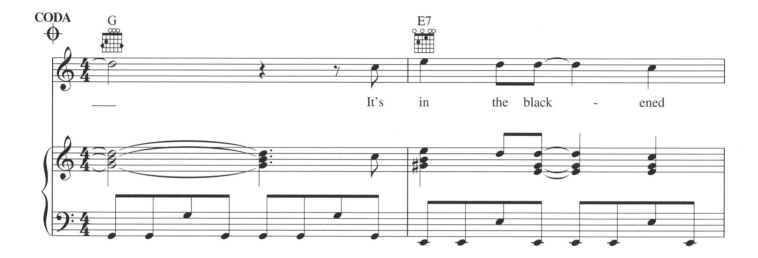

CODA

It's in the black - ened

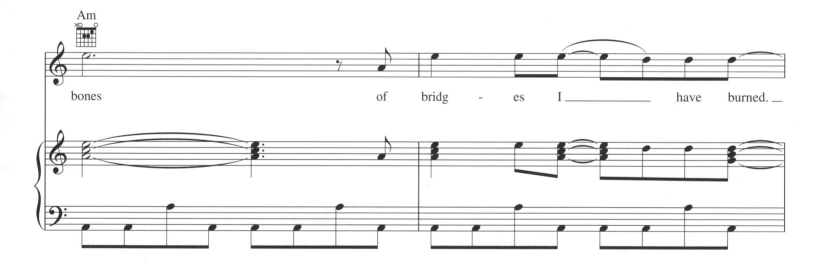

bones of bridg - es I _____ have burned. __

__ So don't a - pol - o - gize, __

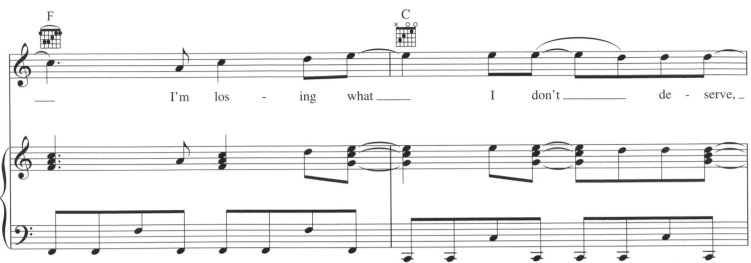

I'm los - ing what ___ I don't ___ de - serve, ___

what I don't _ de - serve. ___

Vocal tacet on repeats

guitar solo

1, 2

3

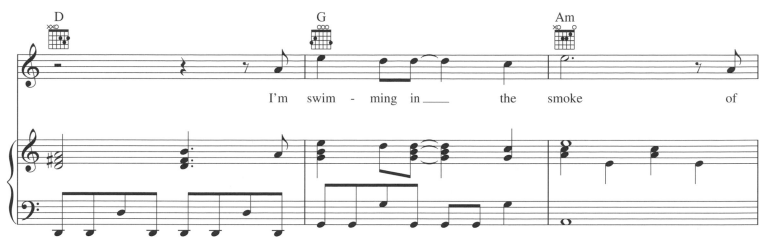

I'm swim - ming in ____ the smoke of

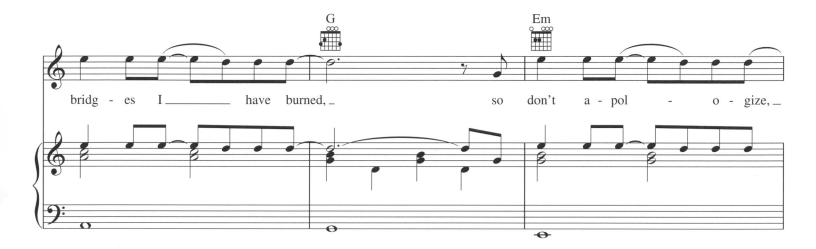

bridg - es I _____ have burned, _ so don't a - pol - o - gize, _

_ I'm los - ing what ___ I don't ____ de - serve. _ The

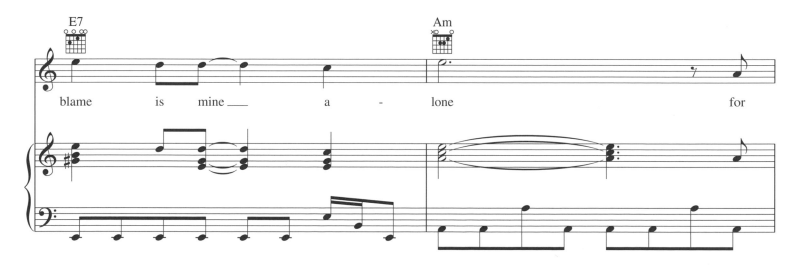

blame is mine ___ a - lone for

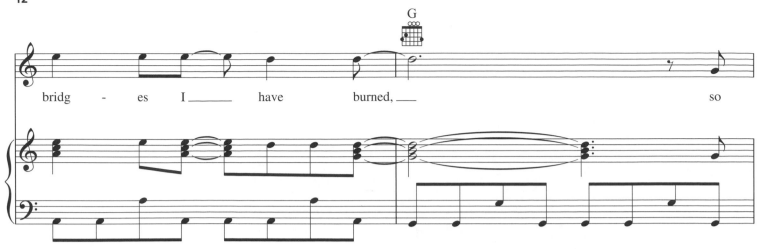

bridg - es I ___ have burned, ___ so

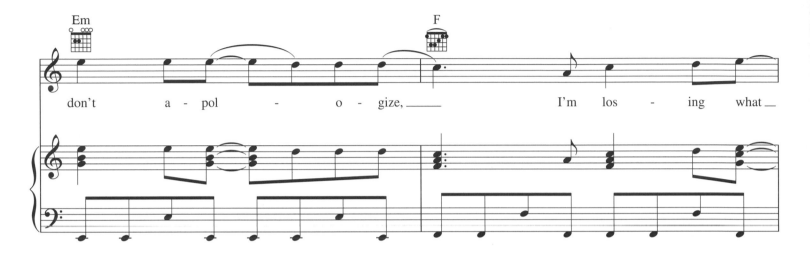

don't a - pol - o - gize, ___ I'm los - ing what ___

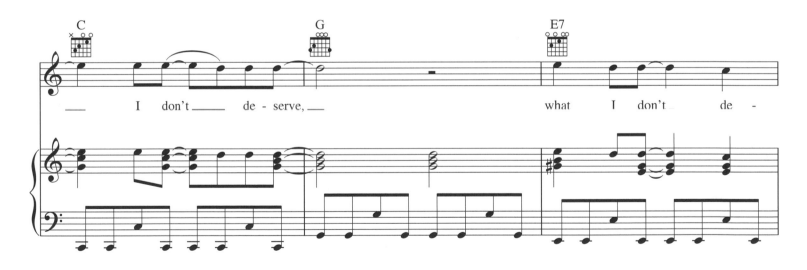

___ I don't ___ de - serve, ___ what I don't de -

serve. ___

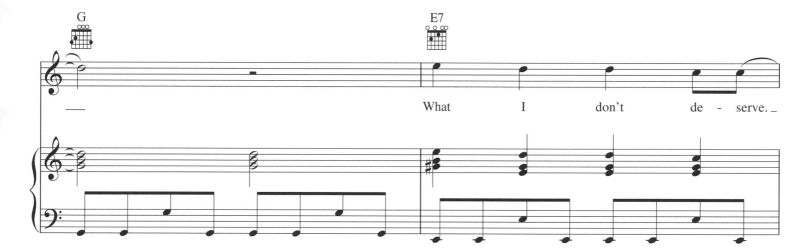

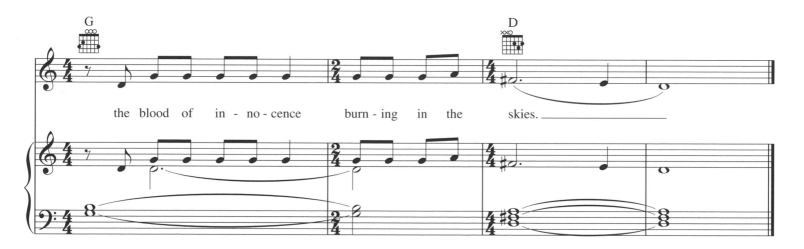

WHEN THEY COME FOR ME

Words and Music by CHESTER BENNINGTON,
ROBERT BOURDON, BRAD DELSON,
DAVE FARRELL, JOSEPH HAHN
and MIKE SHINODA

Industrial Hip-Hop

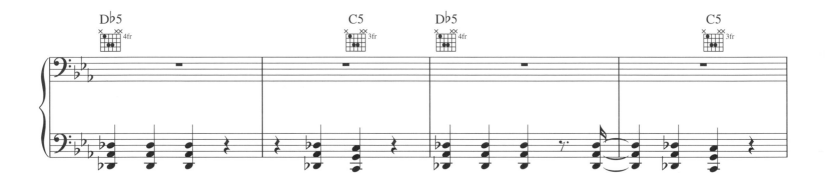

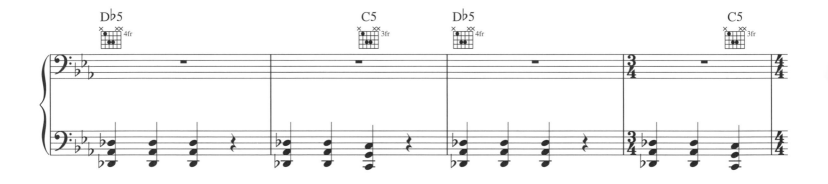

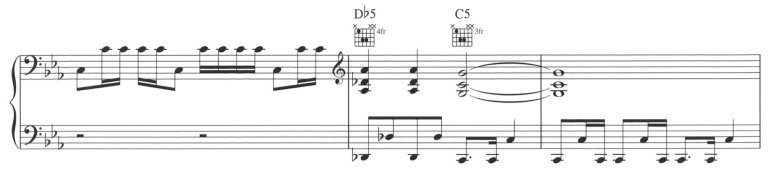

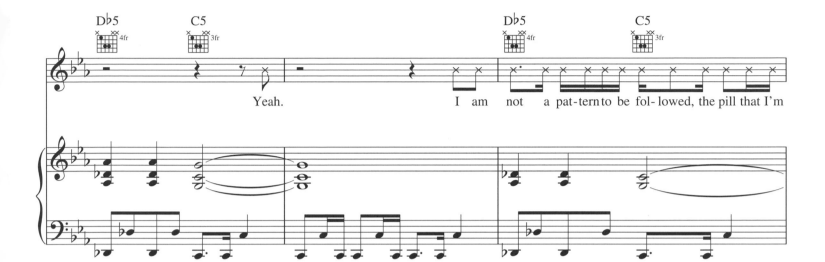

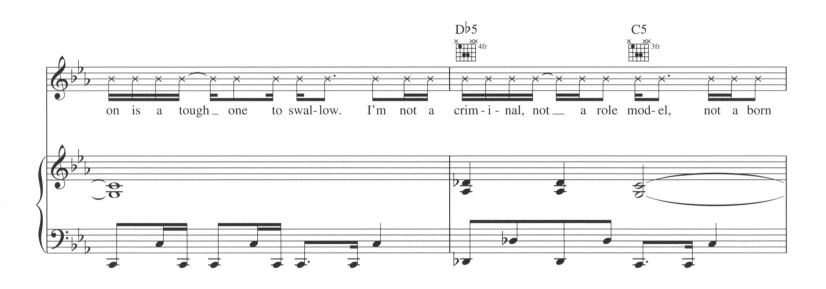

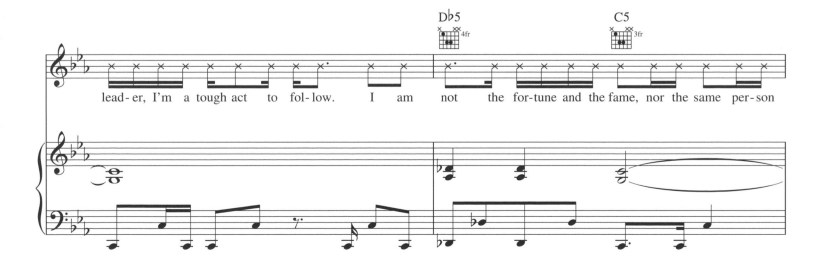

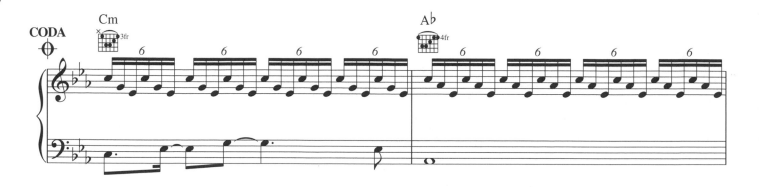

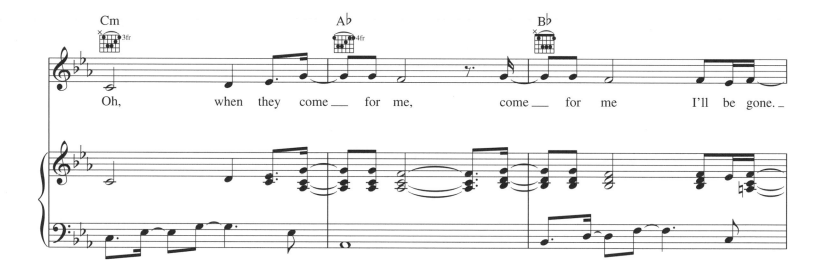

Db5
C5
Ah.
To Coda
Db5
C5
Lau-ren said mon-ey change a sit-u-a-tion,
Big said it in-crease the comp-li-ca-tion.
Db5
C5
Kayne said don't stab, I ain't the one,
Chuck said that U-ZI weighed a moth-er fuck-ing ton.
Db
Cm
And I'm just a stu-dent of the game that they taught me,
4fr
3fr

Oh, when they come ___ for me, come ___ for me I'll be gone. ___

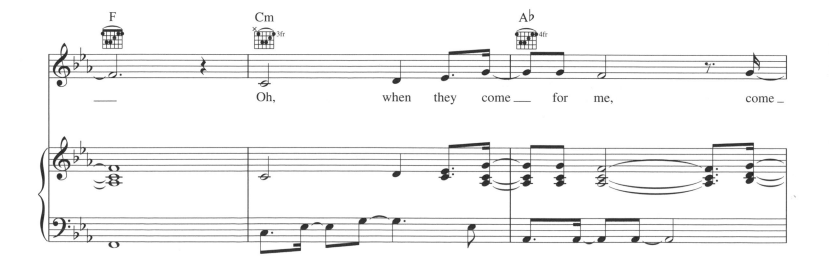

___ Oh, when they come ___ for me, come ___

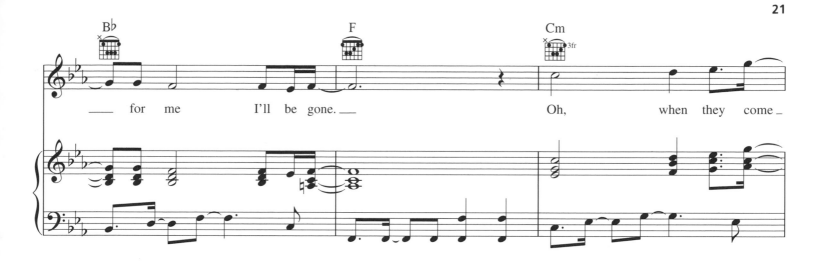

for me I'll be gone. Oh, when they come

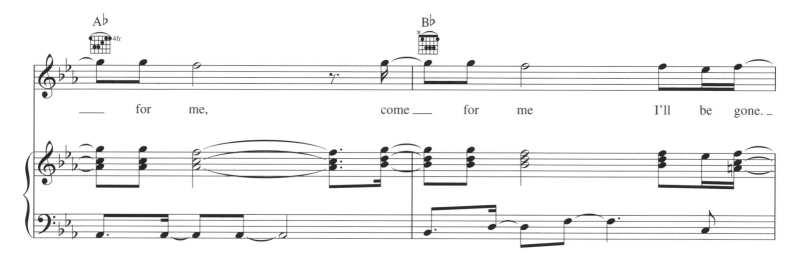

for me, come for me I'll be gone.

And all the peo-ple say... Ah.

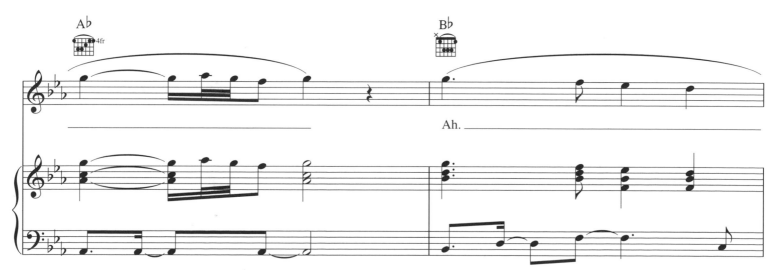

Ah.

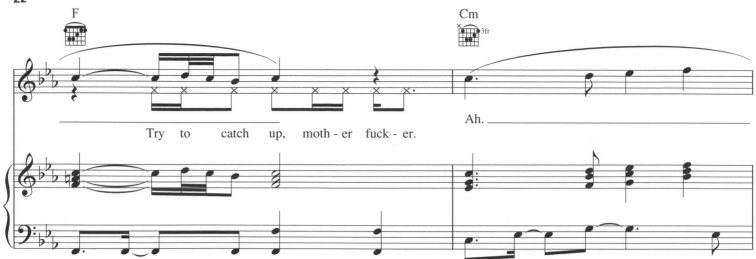

Try to catch up, moth-er fuck-er.

Ah.

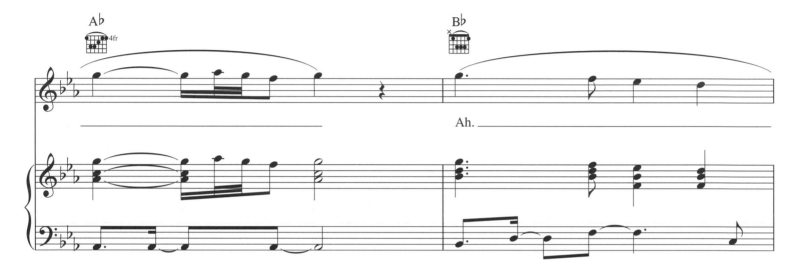

Ah.

And all the peo-ple say...

Ah.

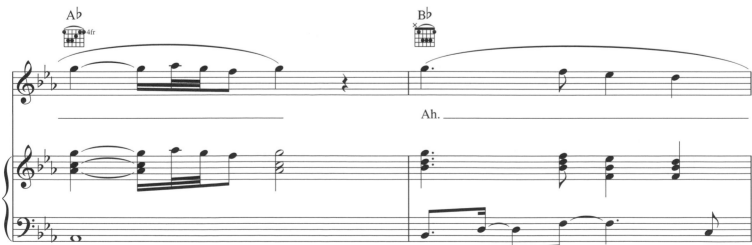

Ah.

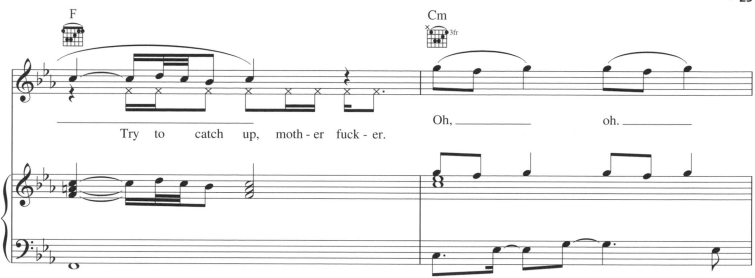

Try to catch up, moth-er fuck-er.   Oh, _____   oh. _____

Ah. _____

Ah. _____   **Play 3 times**

ROBOT BOY

Words and Music by CHESTER BENNINGTON,
ROBERT BOURDON, BRAD DELSON,
DAVE FARRELL, JOSEPH HAHN
and MIKE SHINODA

Epic Ballad

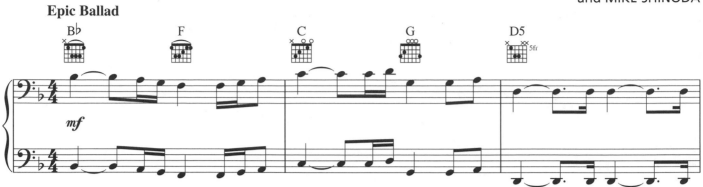

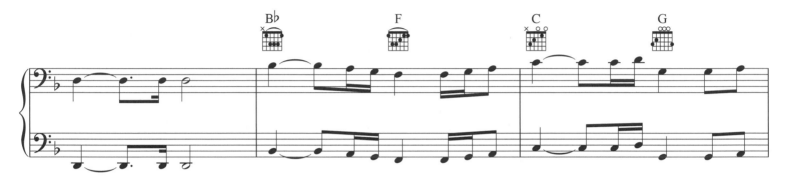

Ooh. _____

You ___ say, you're not gon-na fight 'cause no one will fight for you. _

___ And

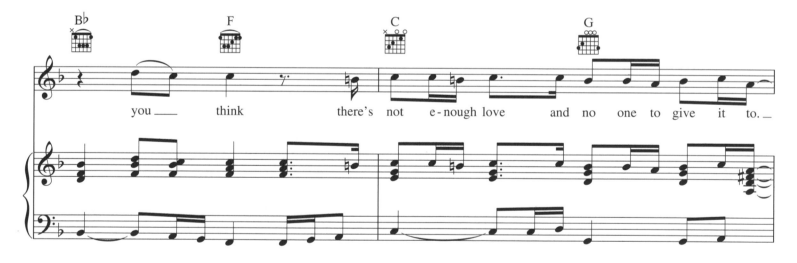

you ___ think there's not e-nough love and no one to give it to. _

___ And

you're _ sure   you've heard for so long   you've got noth-ing left to lose. _

So

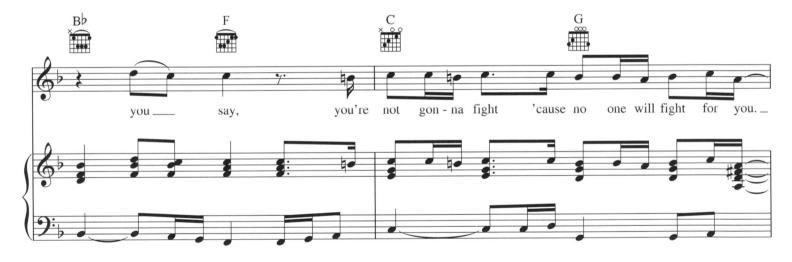

you _ say,   you're not gon-na fight 'cause no one will fight for you. _

You _ say the

weight of the world has kept you from let - ting go. ____ And

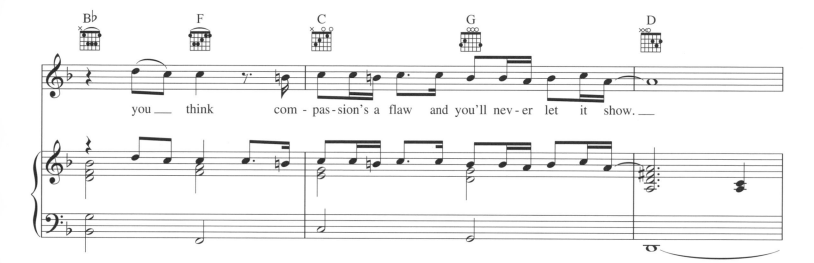

you ___ think com - pas - sion's a flaw and you'll nev - er let it show. __

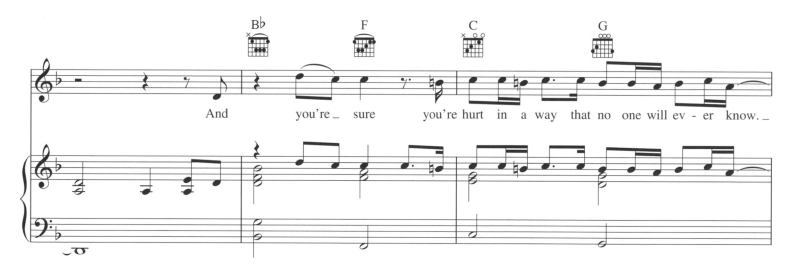

And you're __ sure you're hurt in a way that no one will ev - er know. __

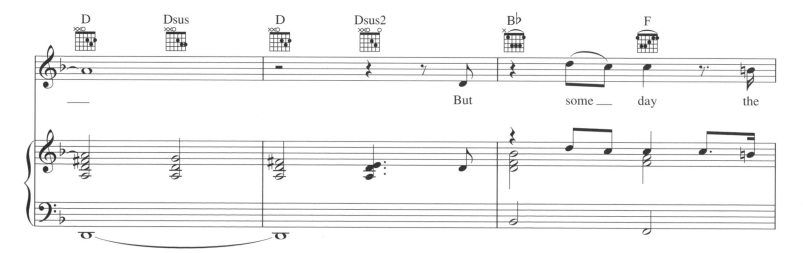

But some ___ day the

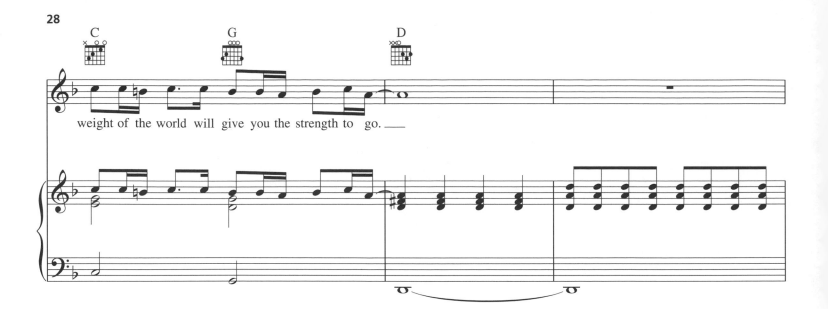

weight of the world will give you the strength to go. ___

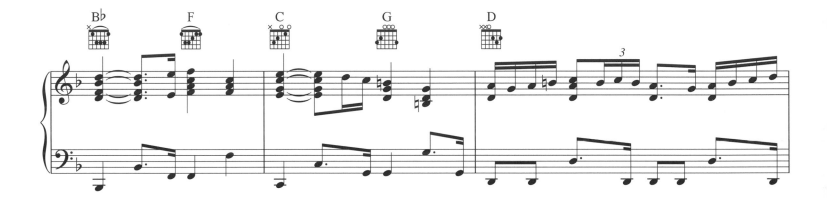

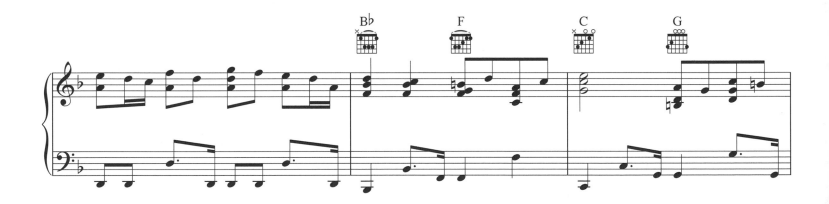

Hold ___ on, the weight of the world will give you the strength to go. __

___ So

hold ___ on, the weight of the world will give you the strength to go. __

___ So

hold ___ on, the weight of the world will give you the strength to go. ___

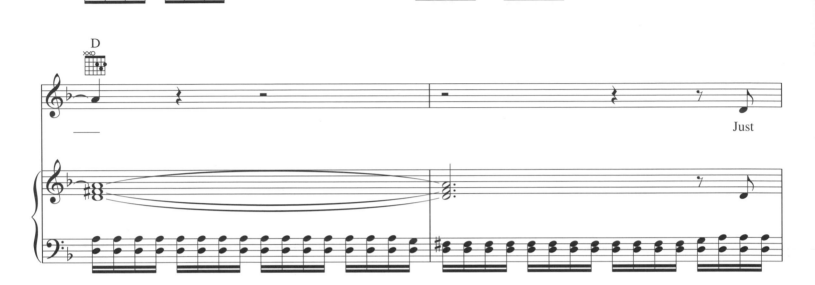

Just

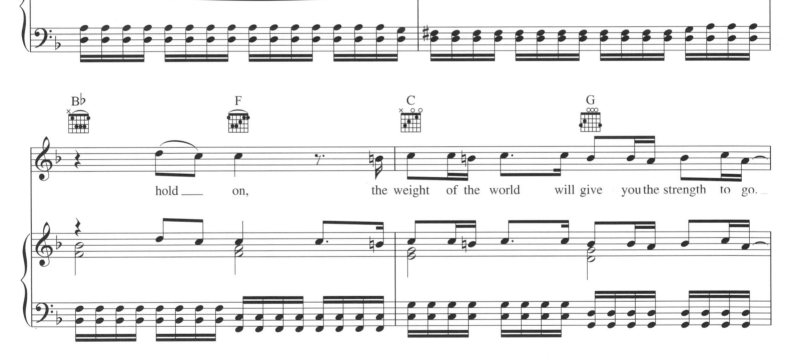

hold ___ on, the weight of the world will give you the strength to go.

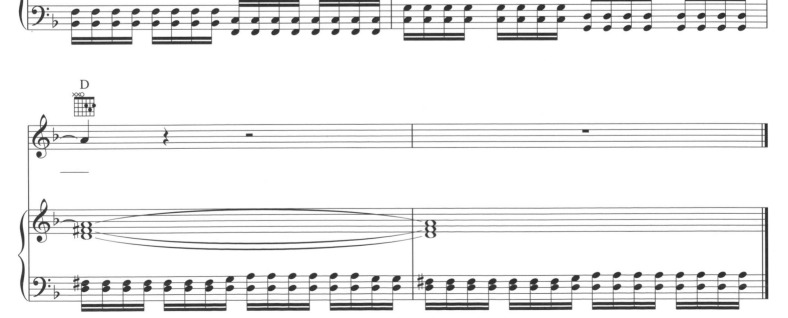

JORNADA DEL MUERTO

Words and Music by CHESTER BENNINGTON,
ROBERT BOURDON, BRAD DELSON,
DAVE FARRELL, JOSEPH HAHN
and MIKE SHINODA

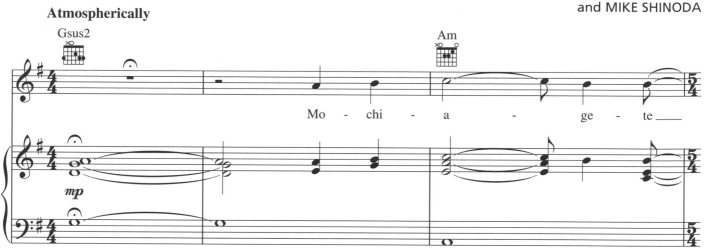

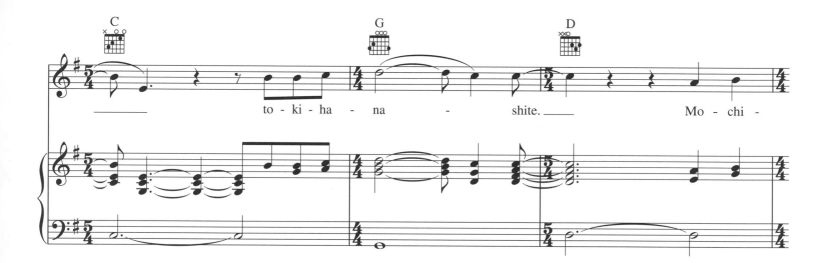

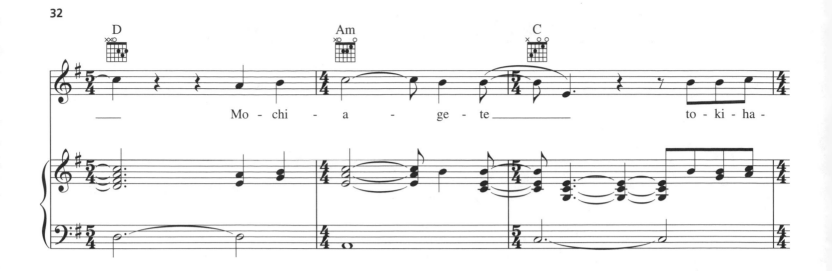

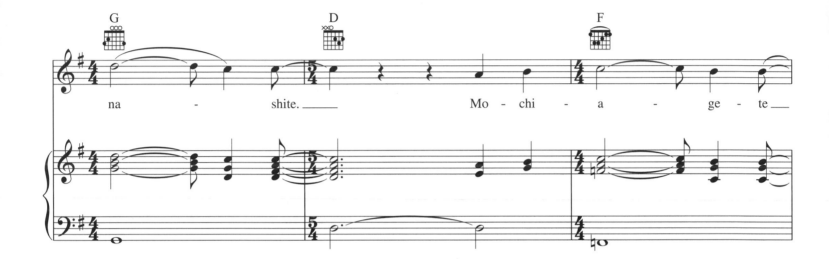

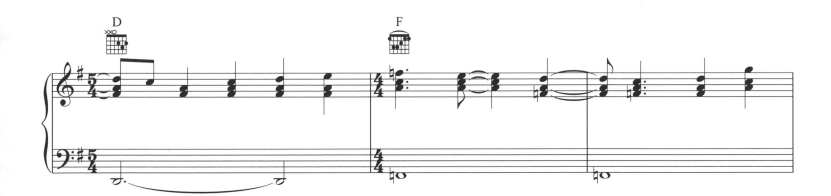

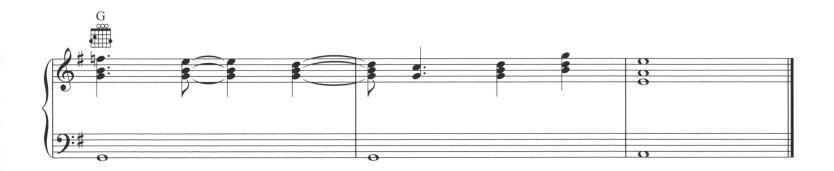

WAITING FOR THE END

Words and Music by CHESTER BENNINGTON,
ROBERT BOURDON, BRAD DELSON,
DAVE FARRELL, JOSEPH HAHN
and MIKE SHINODA

With a moderate groove

liv-ing at the mer-cy of the pain and the fear __ un-til we dead it, for-get it, let it all dis-ap-pear, yeah.

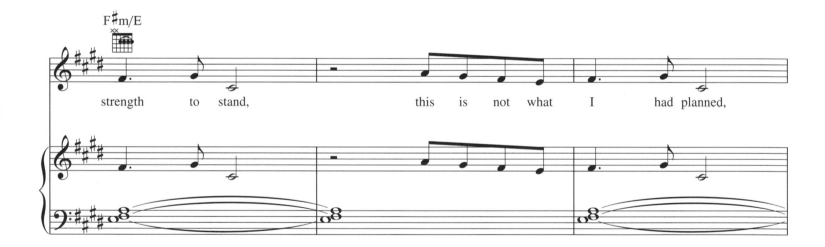

Wait-ing for the end ____ to come, ____ wish-ing I had

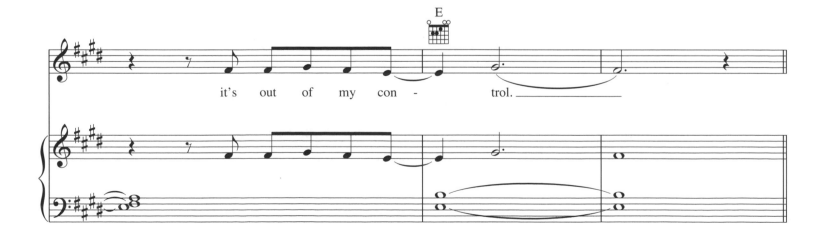

strength to stand, this is not what I had planned,

it's out of my con - trol. ____

Fly - ing at the speed of light, _____ thoughts were spin - ning
Sit - ting in an emp - ty room, _____ try - ing to for -

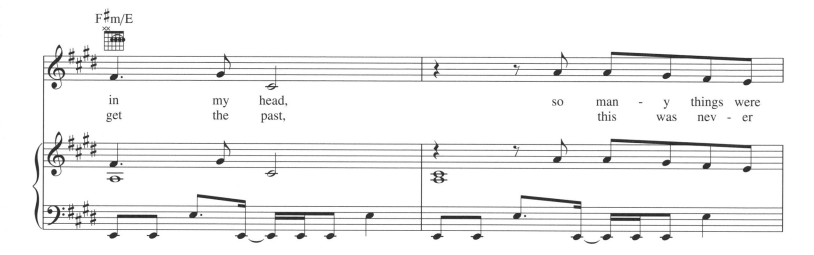

in my head, so man - y things were
get the past, this was nev - er

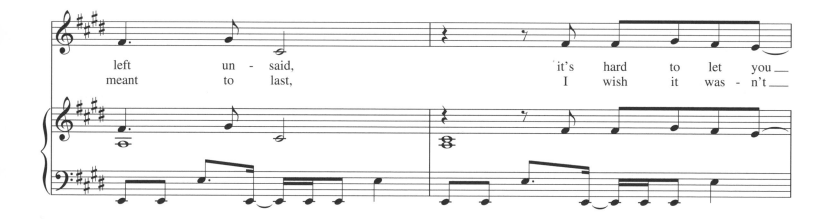

left un - said, it's hard to let you _____
meant to last, I wish it was - n't _____

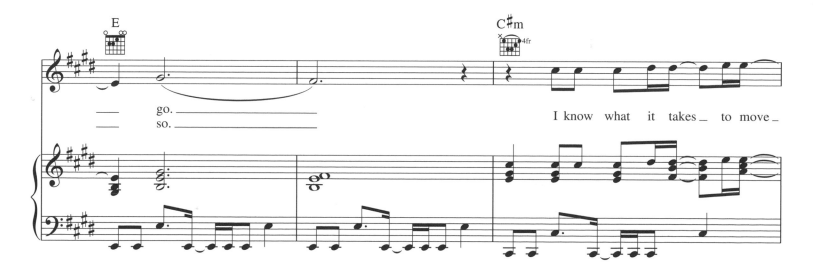

_____ go. _____
_____ so. _____
I know what it takes _ to move _

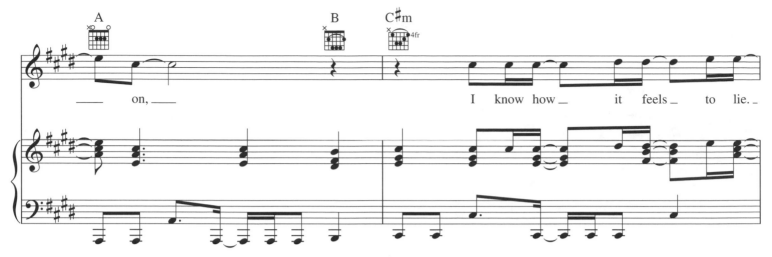

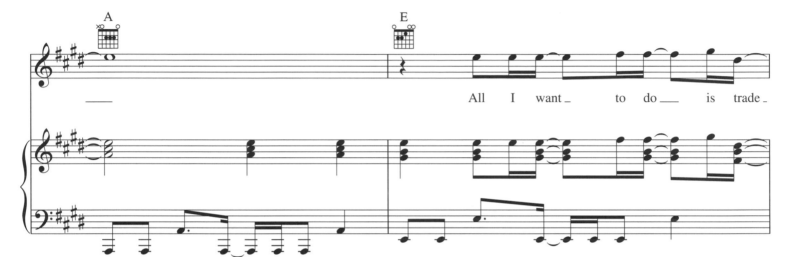

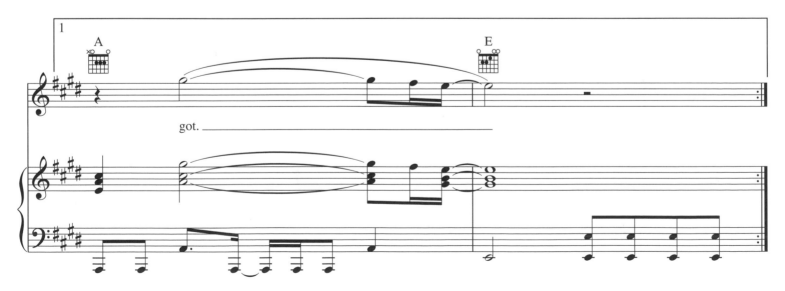

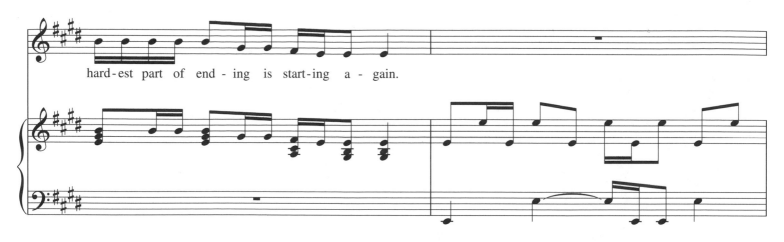

hard-est part of end - ing is start-ing a - gain.

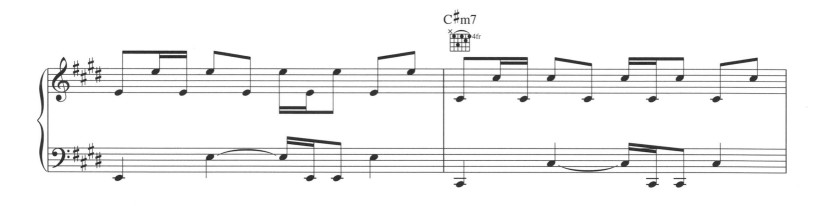

All I want _ to do _ is trade _

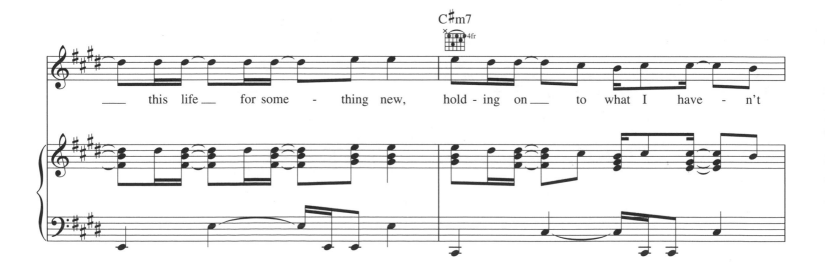

_ this life _ for some - thing new, hold-ing on _ to what I have - n't

got. _____

This is not the end, this is just the be-gin-ning, just a

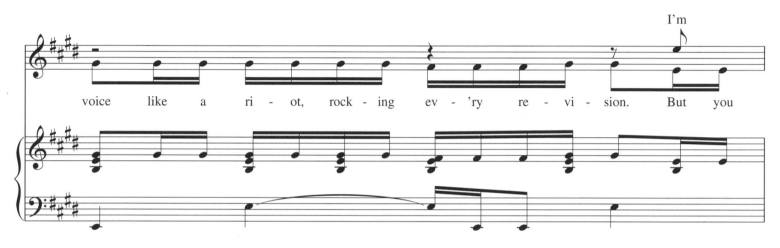

voice like a ri-ot, rock-ing ev-'ry re-vi-sion. But you

I'm

C#m7

hold-ing on _____ to what I have-n't

lis-ten to the tone and the vi-o-lent rhy-thm and though the

A

got. _____

words sound stea-dy, some-thing emp-ty's with-in 'em. We say

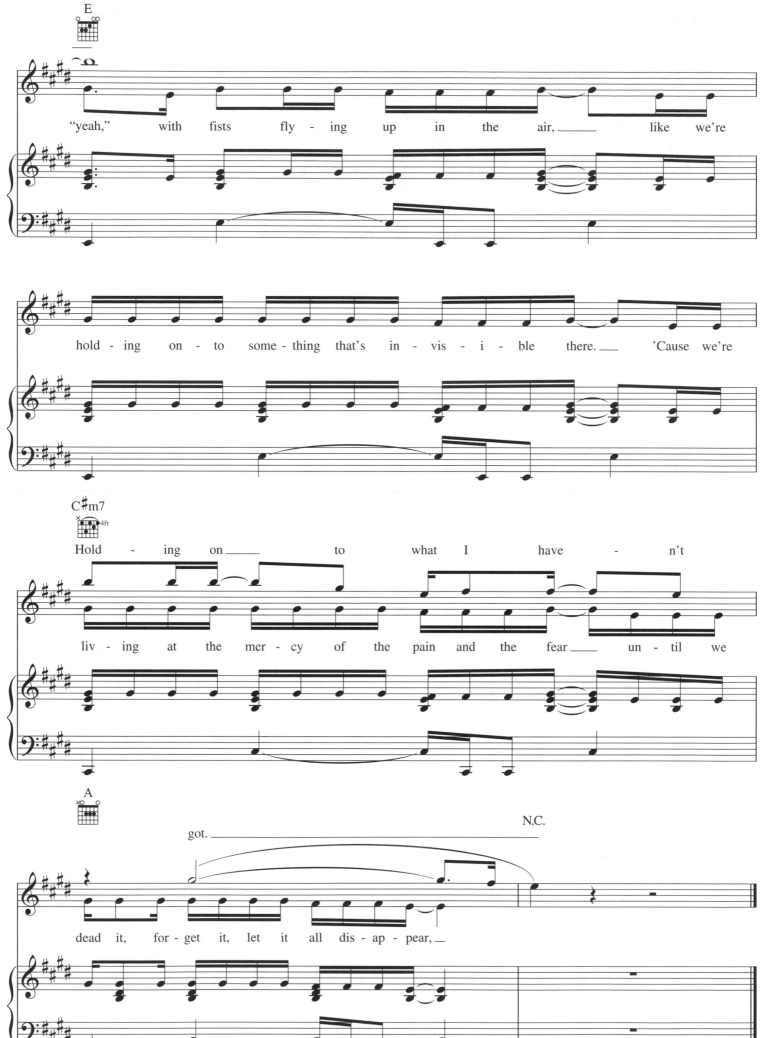

BLACKOUT

Words and Music by CHESTER BENNINGTON,
ROBERT BOURDON, BRAD DELSON,
DAVE FARRELL, JOSEPH HAHN
and MIKE SHINODA

Intense Industrial Rock

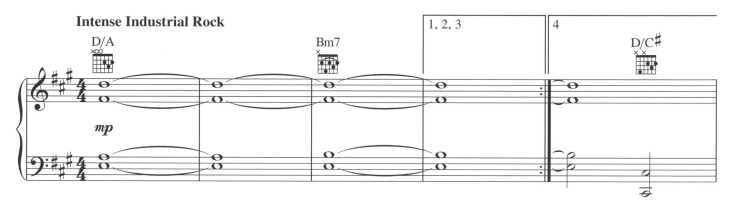

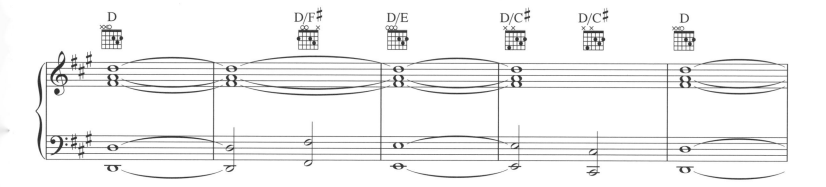

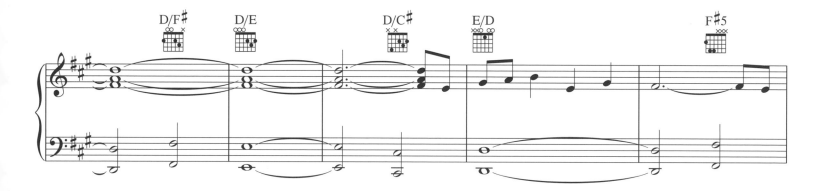

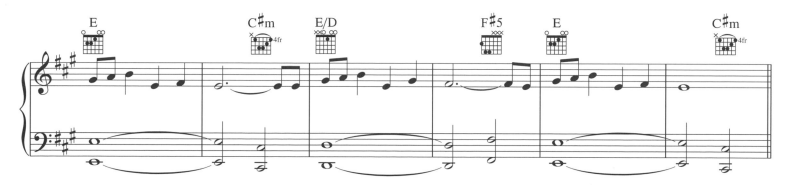

Float-ing down _____ as co-lors fill _____ the light, _____ we

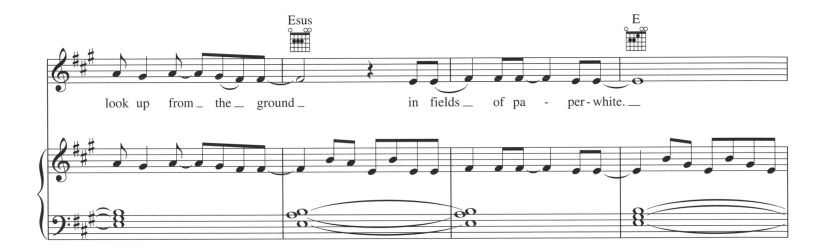

look up from _ the _ ground _ in fields _ of pa - per-white. _

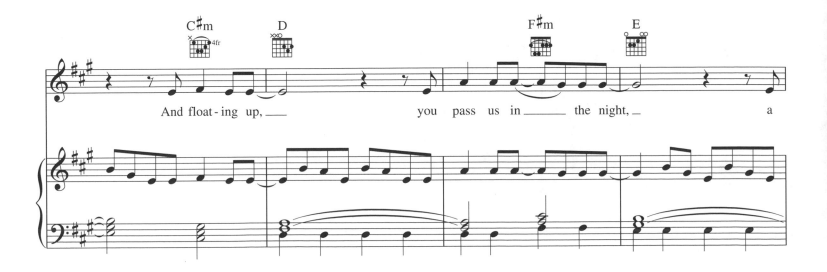

And float-ing up, _____ you pass us in _____ the night, _____ a

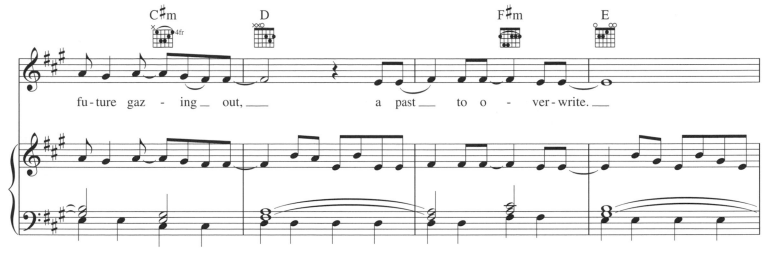

fu - ture gaz - ing_ out, ___ a past ___ to o - ver - write. ___

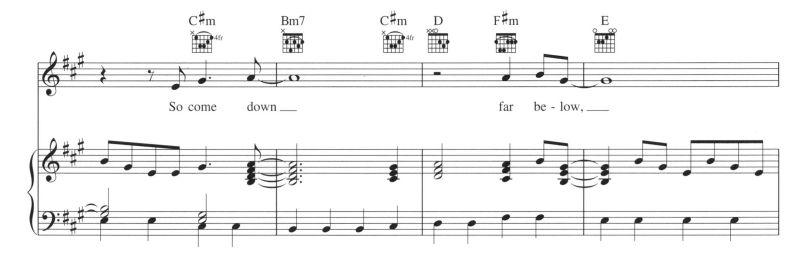

So come down ___ far be - low, ___

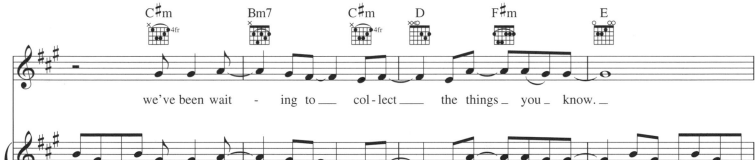

we've been wait - ing to ___ col - lect ___ the things_ you_ know. ___

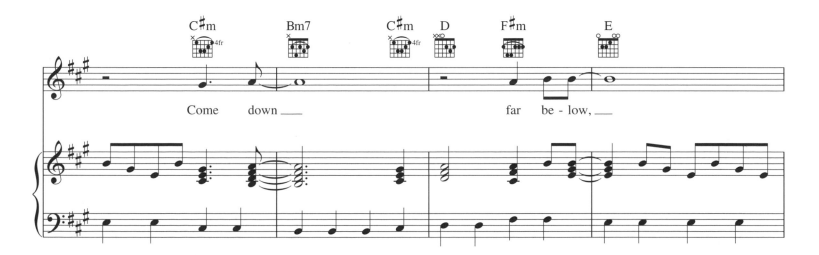

Come down ___ far be - low, ___

WRETCHES AND KINGS

Words and Music by CHESTER BENNINGTON,
ROBERT BOURDON, BRAD DELSON,
DAVE FARRELL, JOSEPH HAHN
and MIKE SHINODA

Industrial Hip-Hop

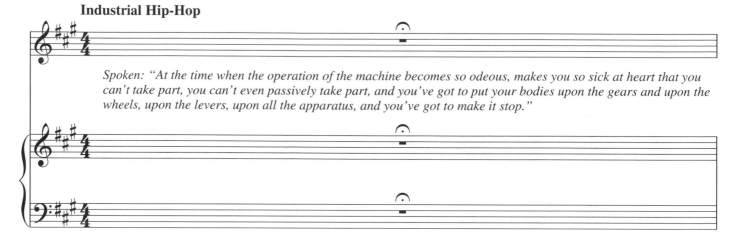

Spoken: "At the time when the operation of the machine becomes so odeous, makes you so sick at heart that you can't take part, you can't even passively take part, and you've got to put your bodies upon the gears and upon the wheels, upon the levers, upon all the apparatus, and you've got to make it stop."

To save

face, how low ___ can you go? Talk a lot of game, but yet ___ you don't know.
pace, how slow ___ can you go? Talk a lot of shit and yet ___ you don't know.

Stat-ic on the way, make us all say "whoa," the peo-ple up top push the peo-ple down low. Get
Fi - re on the way, make you all say "whoa," the peo-ple up top and the peo-ple down low. Get

down and o - bey ev - 'ry word, stead-y get-ting mine if you have-n't yet heard. Want to
down and I'm run-ning it like that, the front of the at - tack is ex - act - ly where I'm at.

take what I got, don't be ab - surd, don't fight the pow-er, no - bod-y gets hurt. If you
some-where in be -tween the kick and the hi - hat, the pen and the con - tract, the pitch and the con-tact. So get

we the an - i - mals take con - trol. Hear us now, __ clear and true,

1

wretch - es and kings, we __ come for you.

So keep

2

wretch - es and kings, we __ come for you.

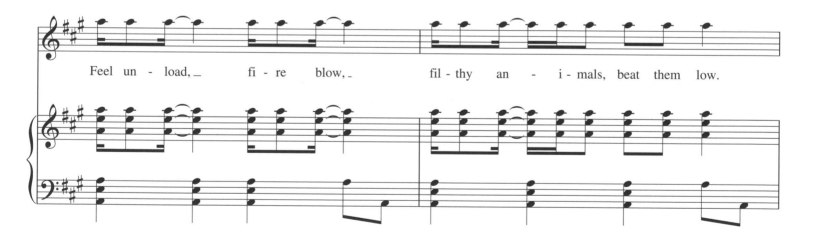

Feel un - load, __ fi - re blow, __ fil - thy an - i - mals, beat them low.

Skin and bone, __ black and blue, no more this sun shall beat on - to you.

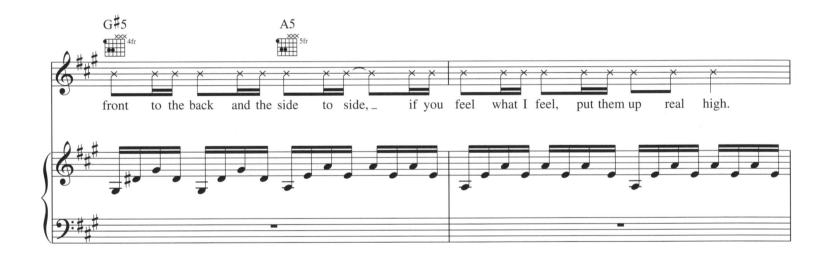

front to the back and the side to side, _ if you feel what I feel, put them up real high.

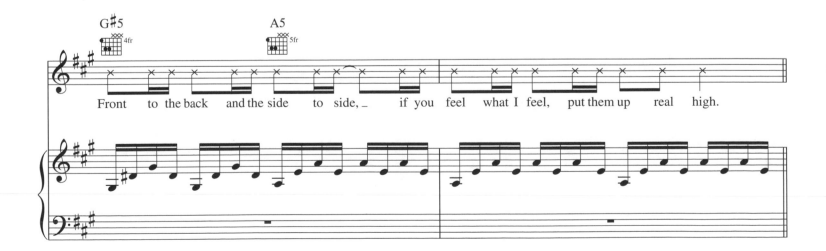

Front to the back and the side to side, _ if you feel what I feel, put them up real high.

WISDOM, JUSTICE, AND LOVE

Words by MARTIN LUTHER KING JR.
Music by CHESTER BENNINGTON,
ROBERT BOURDON, BRAD DELSON,
DAVE FARRELL, JOSEPH HAHN
and MIKE SHINODA

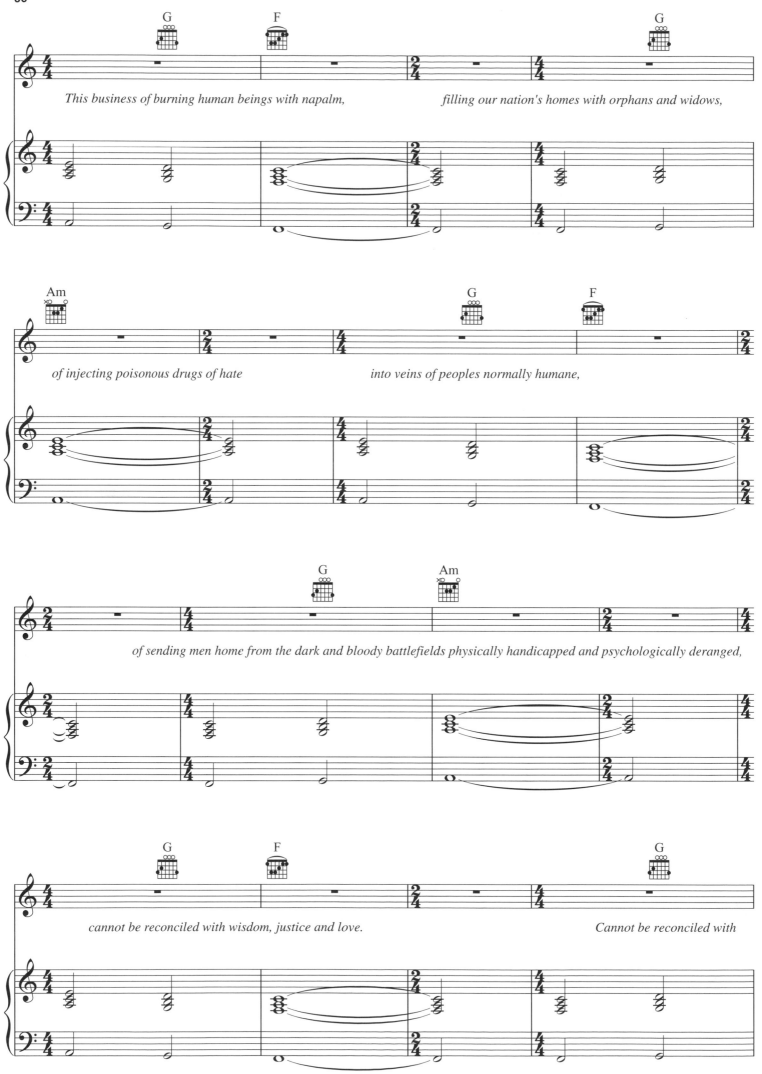

This business of burning human beings with napalm,

filling our nation's homes with orphans and widows,

of injecting poisonous drugs of hate

into veins of peoples normally humane,

of sending men home from the dark and bloody battlefields physically handicapped and psychologically deranged,

cannot be reconciled with wisdom, justice and love.

Cannot be reconciled with

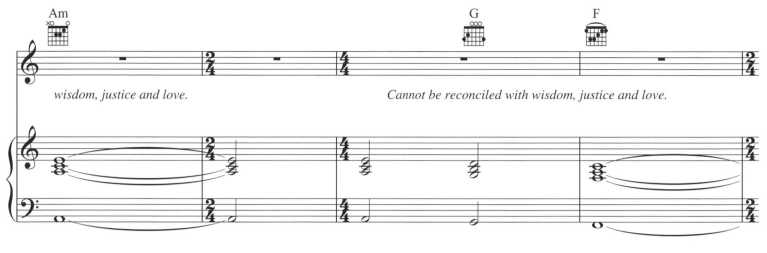

wisdom, justice and love. *Cannot be reconciled with wisdom, justice and love.*

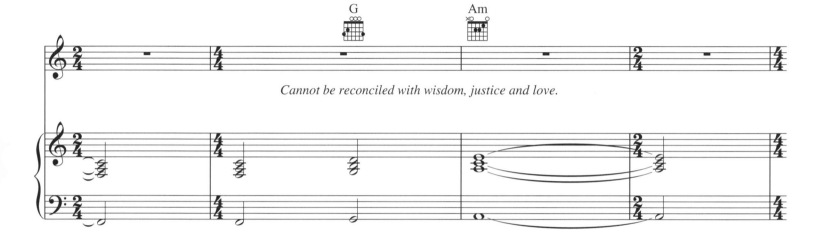

Cannot be reconciled with wisdom, justice and love.

N.C.

Can-not be rec - on - ciled __ with wis - dom, jus - tice and love.

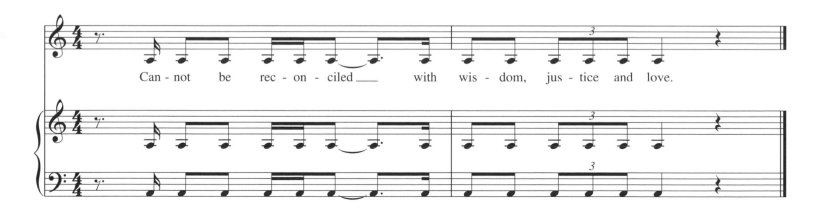

Can - not be rec - on - ciled ____ with wis - dom, jus - tice and love.

IRIDESCENT

Words and Music by CHESTER BENNINGTON,
ROBERT BOURDON, BRAD DELSON,
DAVE FARRELL, JOSEPH HAHN
and MIKE SHINODA

Moderate Pop Rock

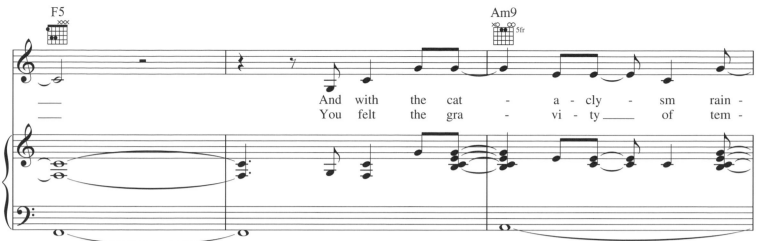

And with the cat - a - cly - sm rain -
You felt the gra - vi - ty ___ of tem -

- ing down, ___ in - sides cry - ing, "Save ___ me, now." ___ You ___
- pered grace ___ fall - ing in - to emp - ty space ___ with no ___

___ were there, ___ im - pos - sib - ly ___ a - lone. ___
___ one there ___ to catch ___ you in ___ their arms. ___

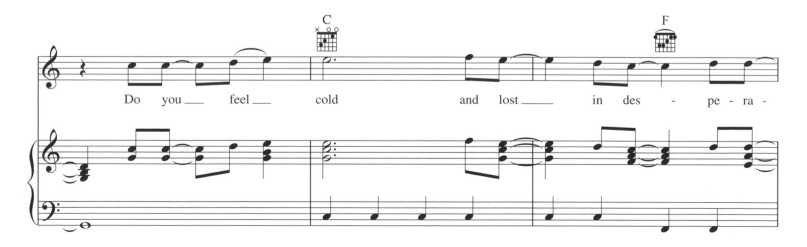

Do you ___ feel ___ cold and lost ___ in des - pe - ra -

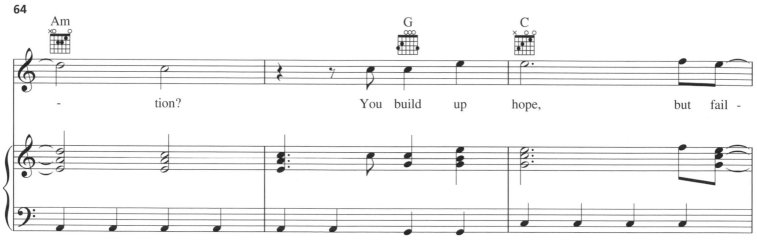

-tion? You build up hope, but fail-

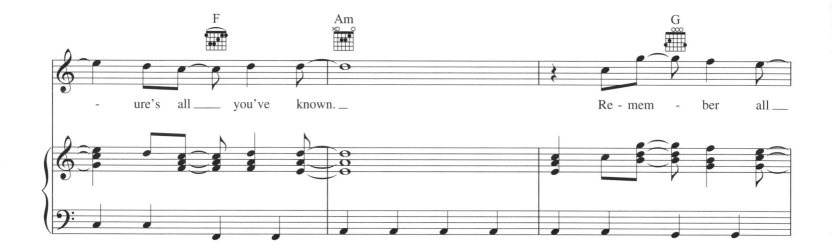

-ure's all ___ you've known. ___ Re- mem - ber all ___

___ the sad - ness and ___ frus - tra - tion and let it

To Coda

go. _____ Let it

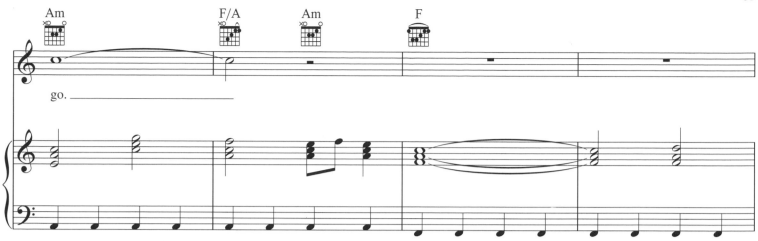

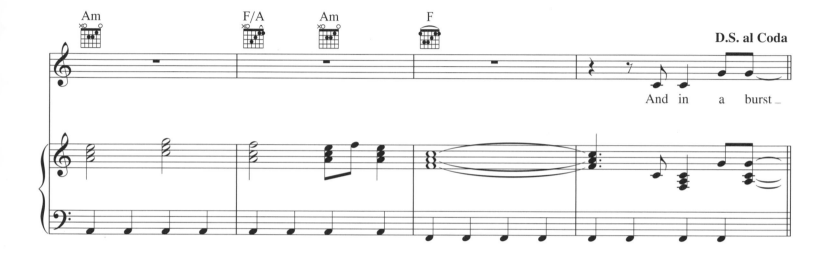

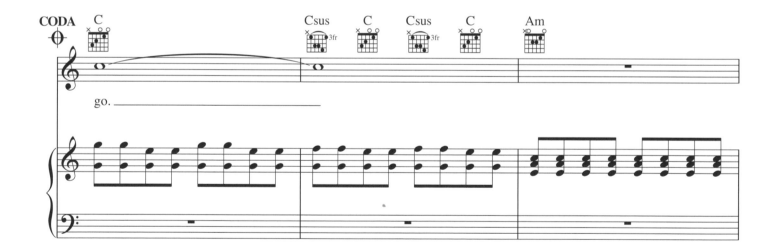

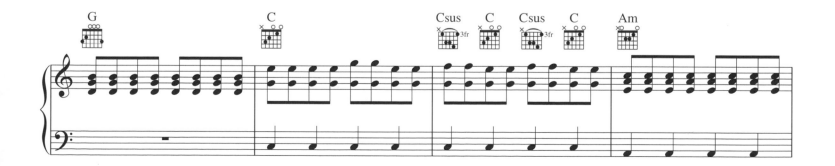

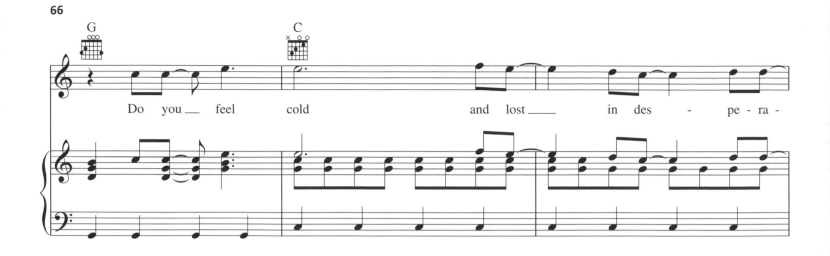

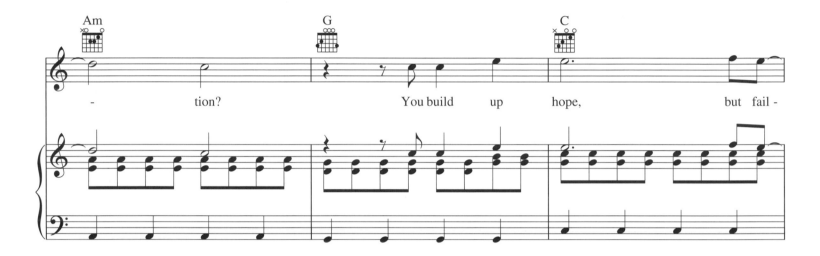

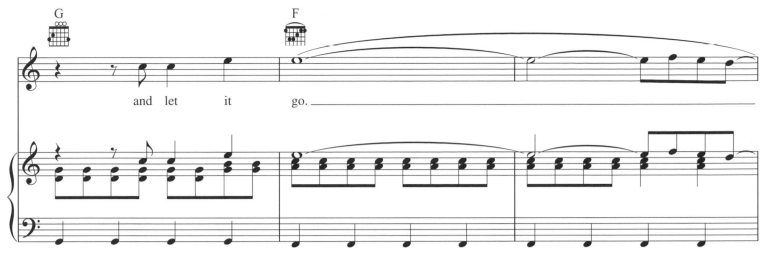

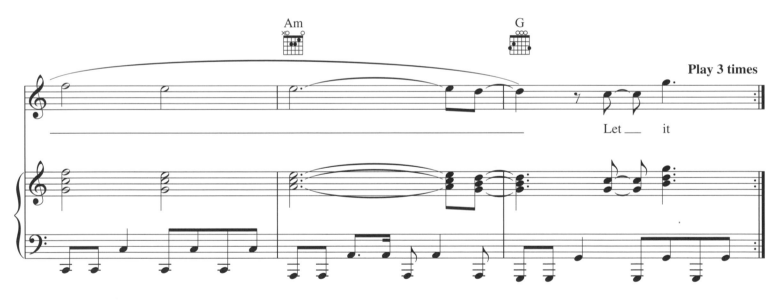

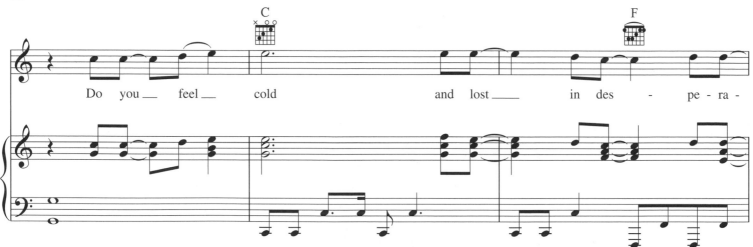

Do you feel cold and lost in des - pe - ra -

- tion? You build up hope, but fail -

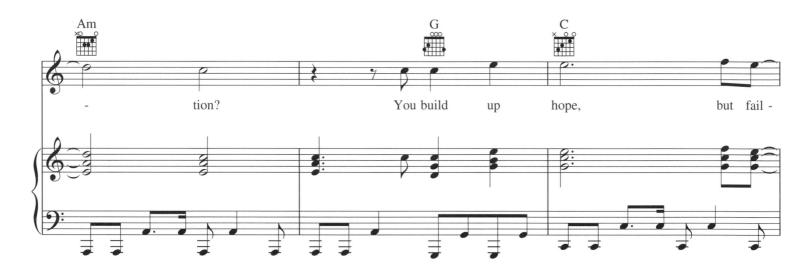

- ure's all you've known. Re - mem - ber all

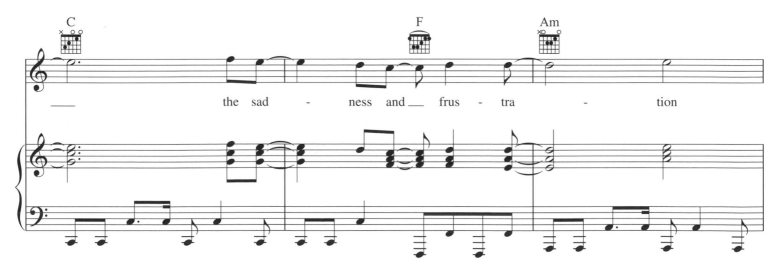

the sad - ness and frus - tra - tion

and let it go. _____

Let it go. _____

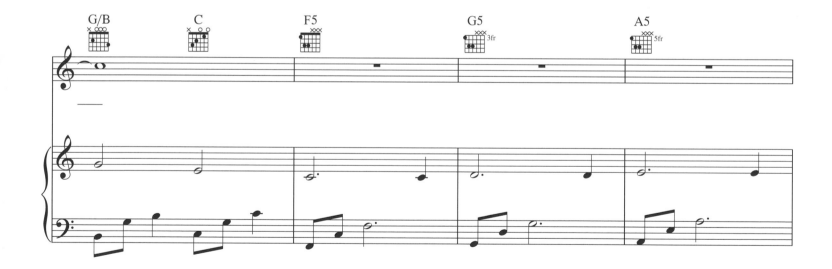

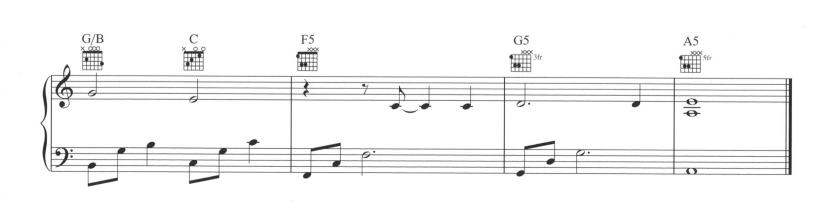

FALLOUT

Words and Music by CHESTER BENNINGTON,
ROBERT BOURDON, BRAD DELSON,
DAVE FARRELL, JOSEPH HAHN
and MIKE SHINODA

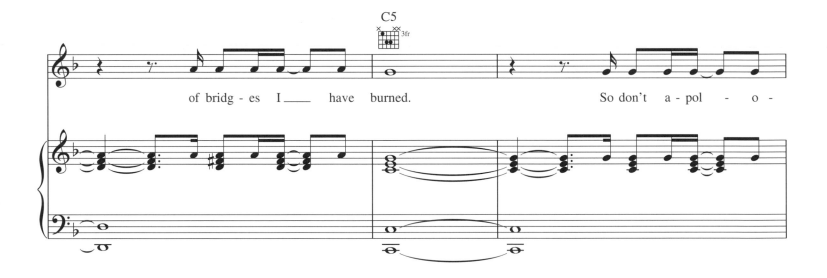

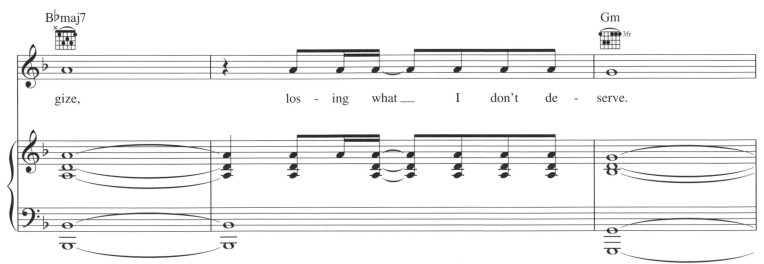

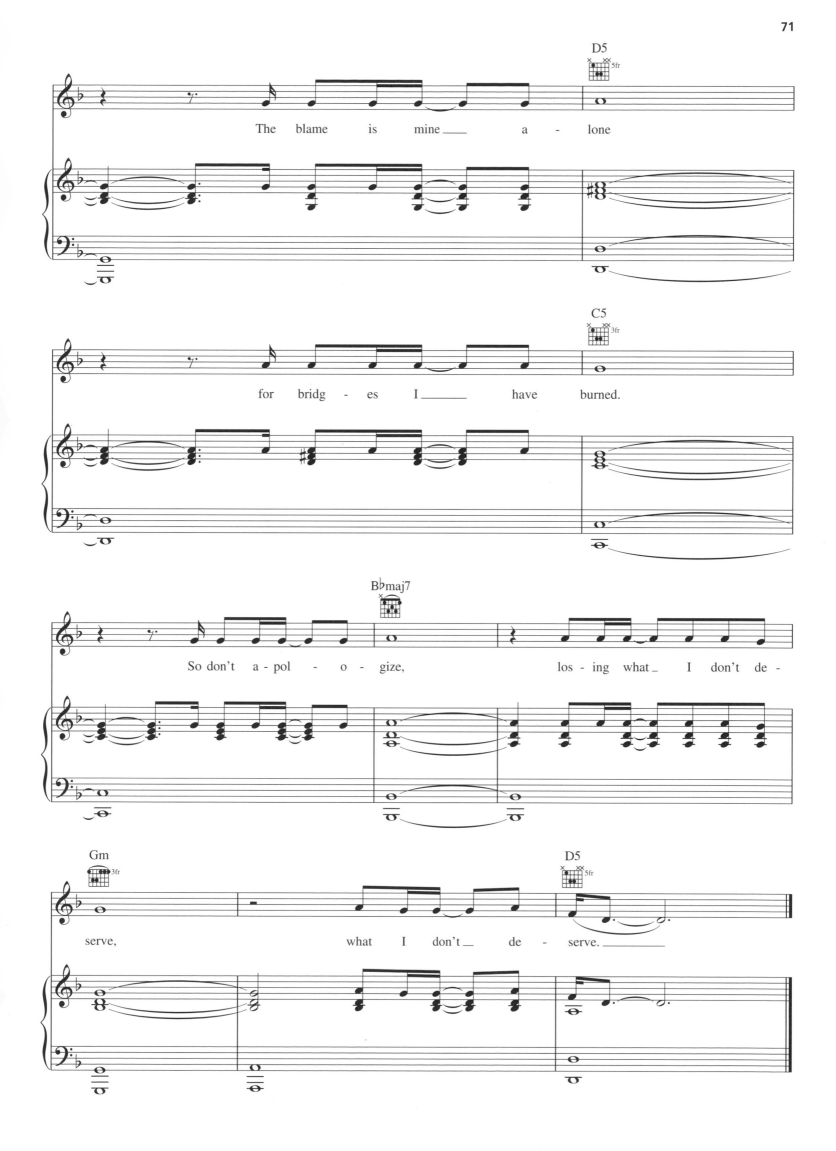

THE CATALYST

Words and Music by CHESTER BENNINGTON,
ROBERT BOURDON, BRAD DELSON,
DAVE FARRELL, JOSEPH HAHN
and MIKE SHINODA

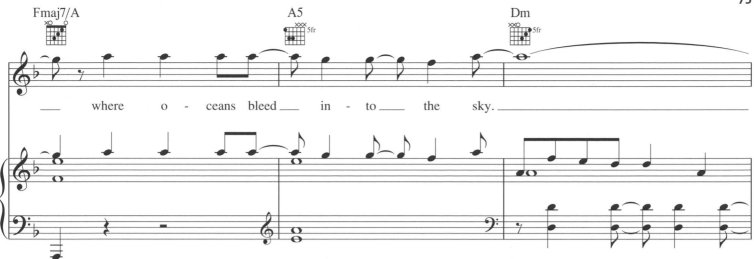

where o - ceans bleed ___ in - to ___ the sky. _____

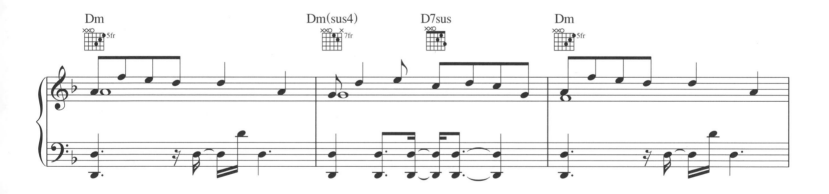

God save us, ev - 'ry one. ___ Will we burn _

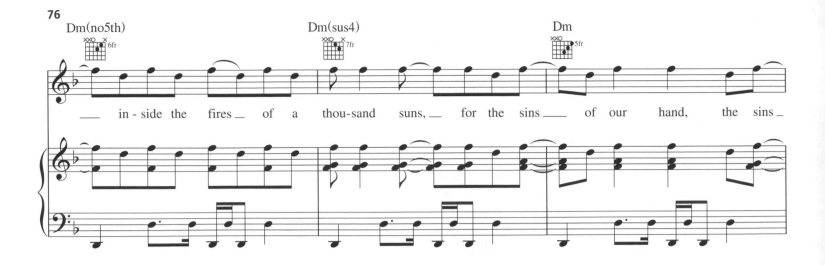

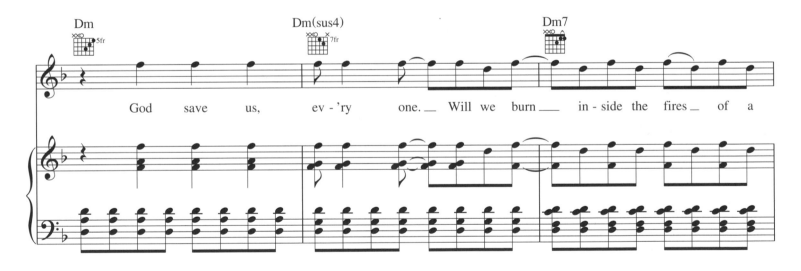

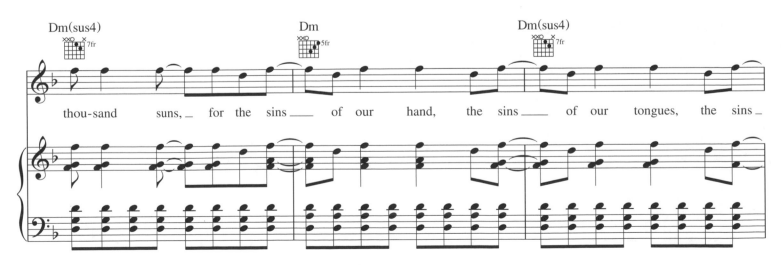

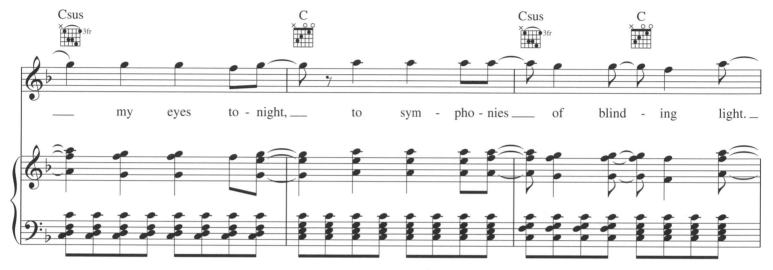

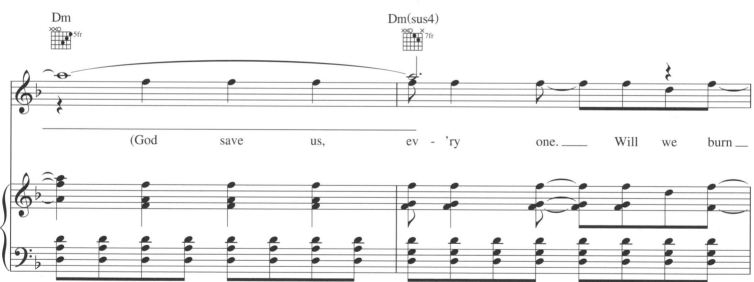

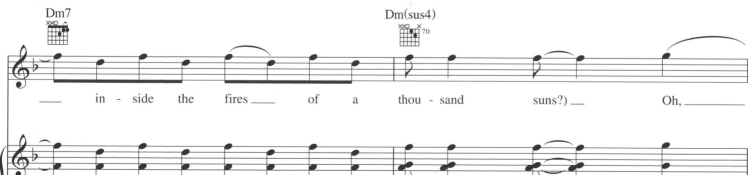

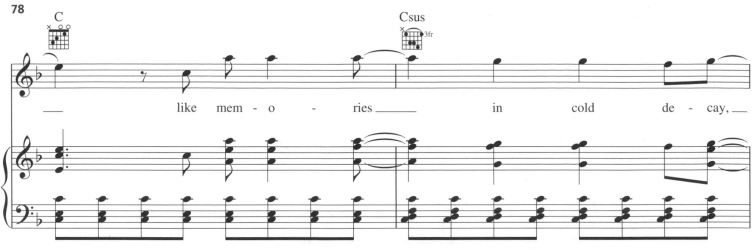

like mem - o - ries _____ in cold de - cay, _____

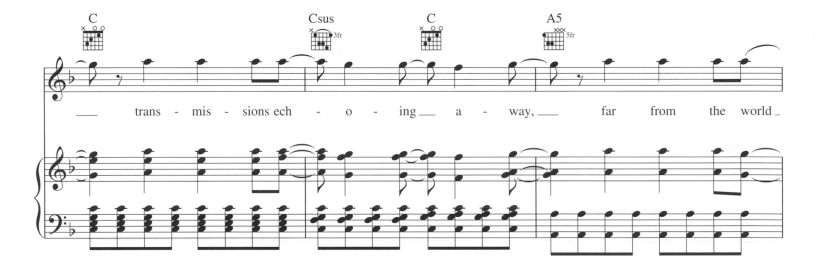

_____ trans - mis - sions ech - o - ing _____ a - way, _____ far from the world _____

_____ with you _____ and I, _____ where o - ceans bleed _____ in - to _____ the sky. _____

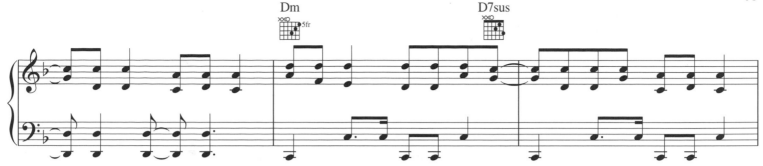

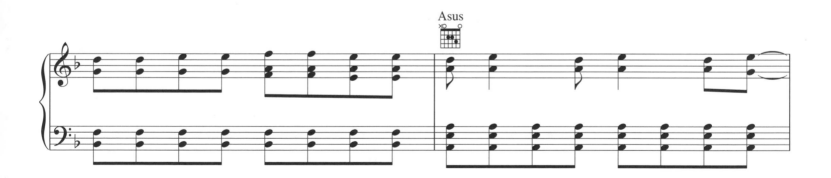

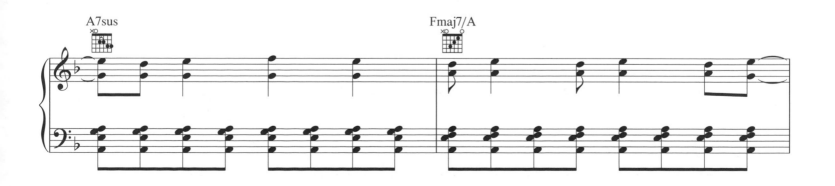

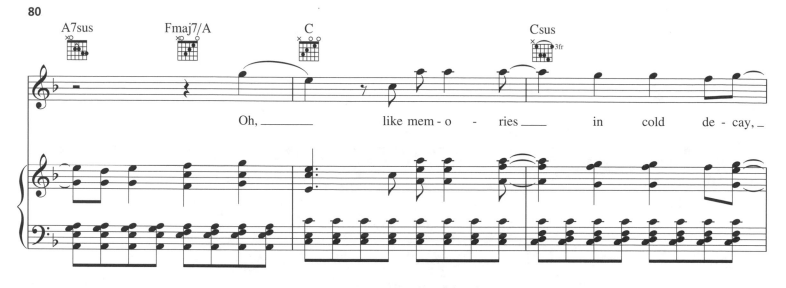

Oh, _____ like mem-o-ries _____ in cold de - cay, _____

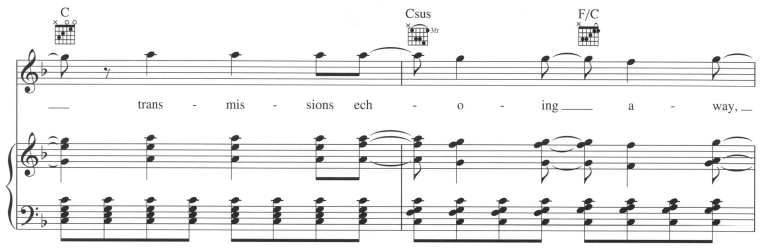

_____ trans - mis - sions ech - o - ing _____ a - way, _____

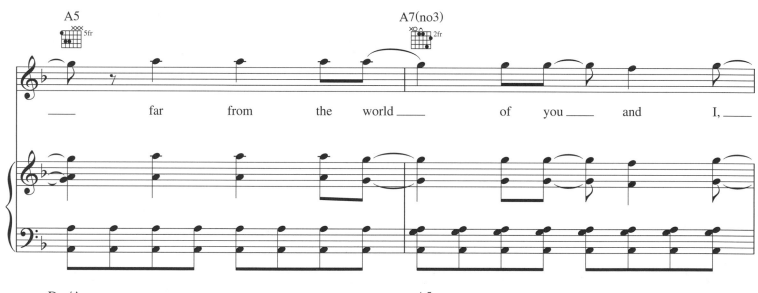

_____ far from the world _____ of you _____ and I, _____

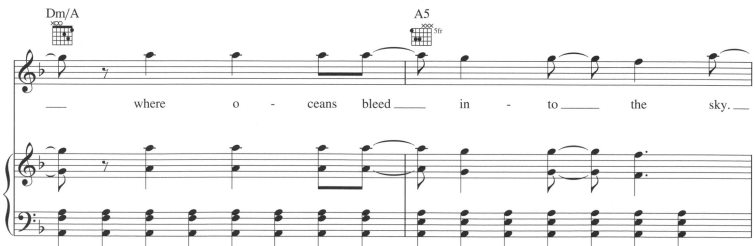

_____ where o - ceans bleed _____ in - to _____ the sky. _____

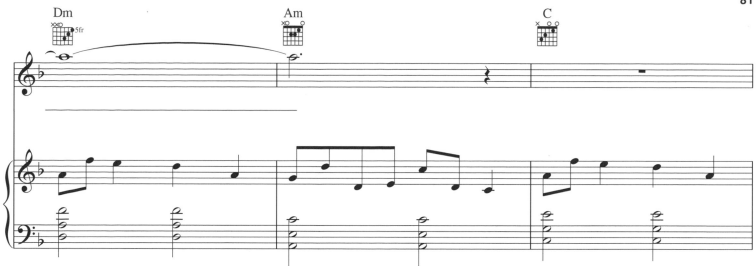

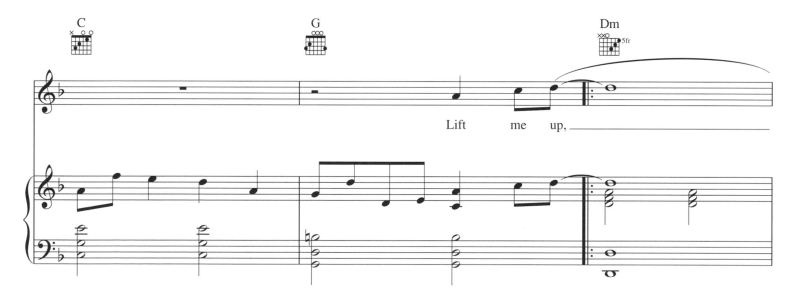

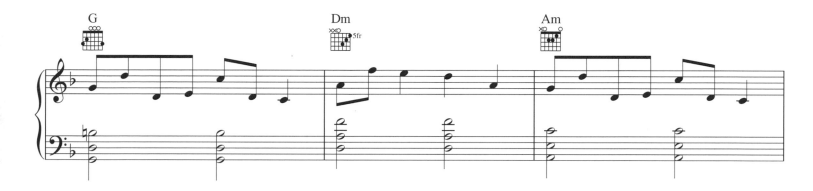

Lift me up, _____

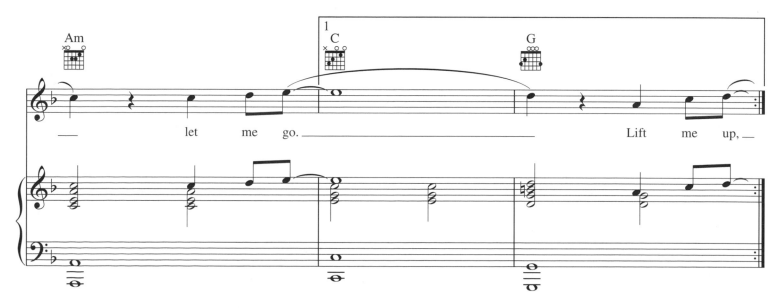

_____ let me go. _____ Lift me up, _____

THE MESSENGER

Words and Music by CHESTER BENNINGTON,
ROBERT BOURDON, BRAD DELSON,
DAVE FARRELL, JOSEPH HAHN
and MIKE SHINODA

Acoustic Ballad

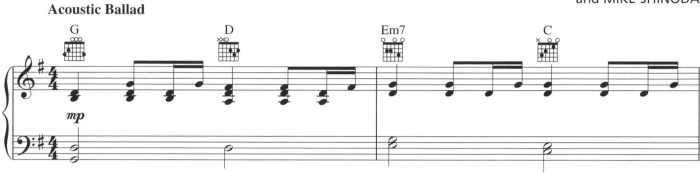

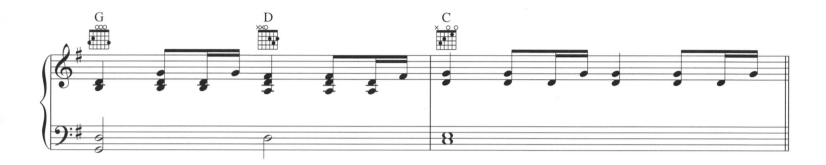

When you feel you're a-lone, __ cut off from this cruel world, __
When you've suf-fered e-nough, __ and your spir-it is break-ing, __

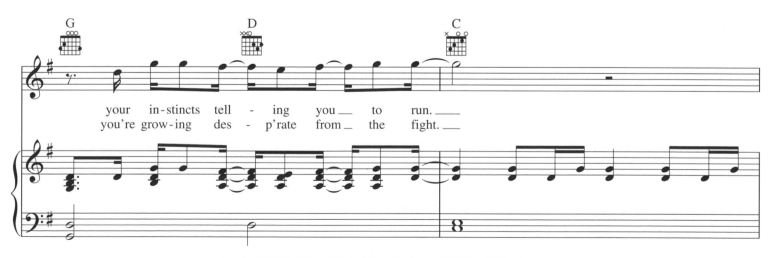

your in-stincts tell-ing you __ to run. __
you're grow-ing des-p'rate from __ the fight. __

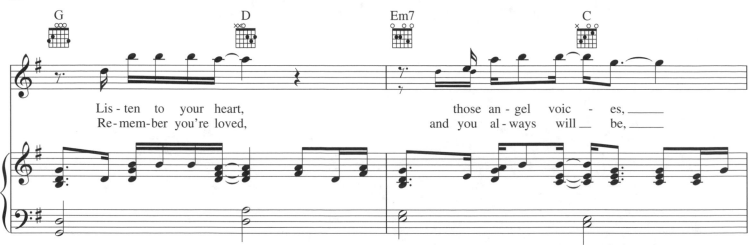

Lis - ten to your heart, those an - gel voic - es, _____
Re - mem - ber you're loved, and you al - ways will __ be, _____

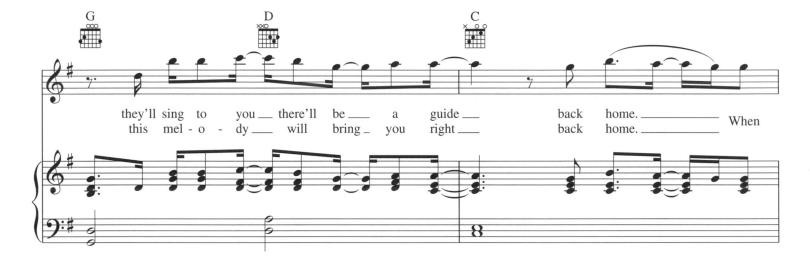

they'll sing to you __ there'll be __ a guide __ back home. _____
this mel - o - dy __ will bring __ you right __ back home. _____ When

life leaves us __ blind, _____

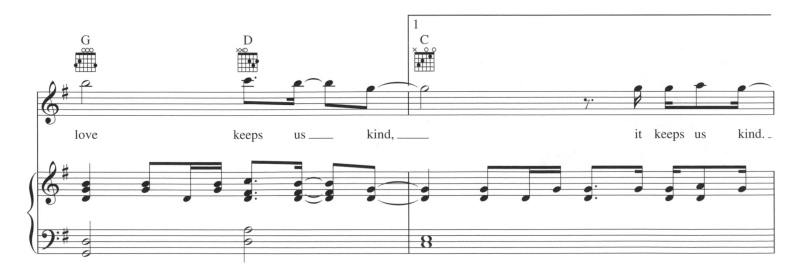

love keeps us __ kind, _____ it keeps us kind. _

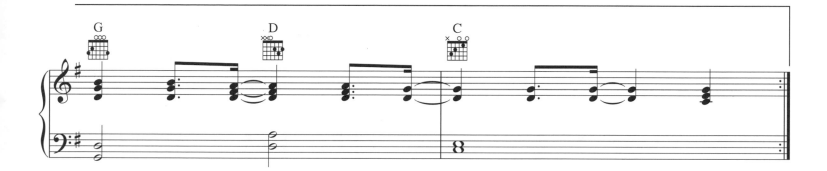

When life leaves __ us ___ blind, ___

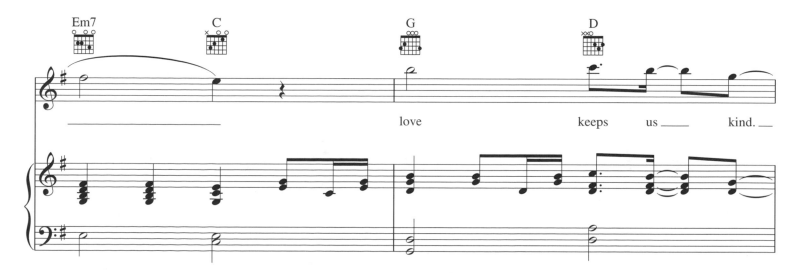

_____ love keeps us ___ kind. __

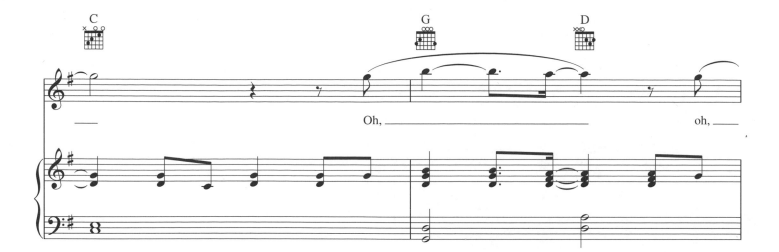

Oh, _____ oh, _____

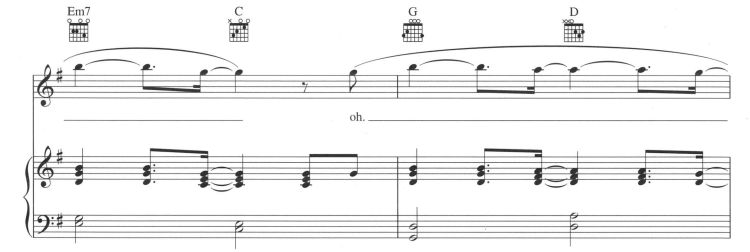

_____ oh. _____

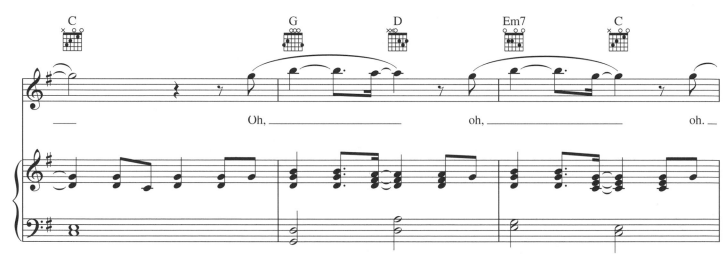

Oh, _____ oh, _____ oh. _

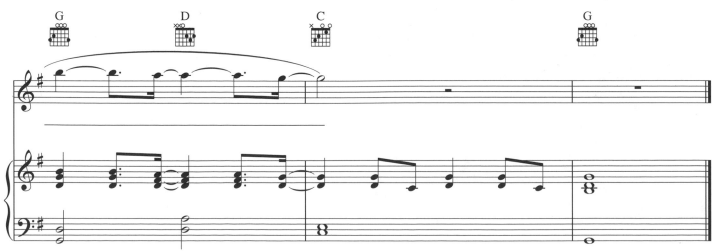